Coloniz

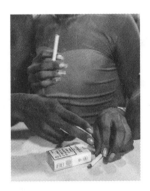

Benjamín Naka-Hasebe Kingsley

Distributed by Independent Publishers Group
Chicago

Saturnalia Books
105 Woodside Rd.
Ardmore, PA 19003
info@saturnaliabooks.com

ISBN: 978-1-947817-02-9
Library of Congress Control Number: 2018910481

Book Design by Robin Vuchnich
Printing by Versa Press
Cover Art: "La Fresa, Cuba LGBT" by Alejandro Cegarra

Distributed by:
Independent Publishing Group
814 N. Franklin St.
Chicago, IL 60610
800-888-4741

Un fuerte abrazo to the journals and anthologies in which many of these poems appeared, sometimes in earlier forms:

Tupelo Press Native Voices: Honoring Indigenous Poetry
Proud to Be: Writing by American Warriors

American Indian Culture and Research Journal
The Asian American Literary Review
Colorado Review
Columbia Poetry Review
Crab Orchard Review
The Georgia Review
International Journal of Indigenous Literature
jubilat
Meridian
Michigan Quarterly Review
the minnesota review
Missouri Review
Ninth Letter
Oxford American
PANK Magazine
Puerto del Sol
Rattle: Poet's Respond
Salamander
The Journal
Tin House
Water-Stone Review
Waxwing
West Branch

In memory of Adrian C. Louis
Onęh go' hya'
Goodbye, for now

Table of Contents

From Nippon refugee

who America caged.

From Onondaga son

who America imprisoned

who they couldn't board into whiteness.

From Rust Belt trailers.

From two wheelbarrow factory workers.

From PA to LA to MIA to out here in West Baltimore.

From counting every penny to carving the love of poems.

From unheard prayers & these answered dreams.

We are here. I am here. I am alive.

—

Our Broke-Ass Ladder of Opportunity
or
The Block Boy Anthem

Streets raised me
I've heard old heads in the complex
say. It ain't true:

                tenant reality was complex
    colonies   a project
after-project
        of stair   wells
our city's stray

              spine
                 of carpet

                         steps
    & clawed doors
          that apartment   hole
            of families in infinite   cells
far behind.

      We grew
         weed quick
   on Wabash Ave
     single stairwell   NO LOITERING signs
be damned
     we shades
of six & seven

years   happy
for forgotten   copper
us browned boys
          penny-rubbed
feather-headed   corn-cropped
          buzzed-down   fro'd-up
                    in new skin us boys raising each other
     onto cardboard sleds
          brown-knuckling
refrigerator boxes zipped   down them steps.
     Our hunger
was the best
     spice.
                                   Flight
     after flight
               of stairs
     zipped no snow   no playground park
          no guardian   who'd give us a gentle push.
We pushed   hard
               daily
          until Cortel unzipped
                         the sleeve
          of his left elbow   hooked that thin trout skin
     on the head   of a nail
                    exposed
wriggling

we saw white

        bone   beneath

the flash

      of ligament twist

      of tears & glittered fish

    line of gums.

Wouldn't be long before

        red &blue would circle round

    slow roll the block with the spangled

         stars of his spotlights

so we flagged

    him street side

      hollered

        Mister! Sir!   for the first time

      cop told us   call 911   but we thought we had.

We thought we had

        for the last time

    until Shawn flew   higher

than any boy could

      from top step

         caught more   air

    than any jet plane

          we'd never ridden in

    an ambulance   before

          the sun turned its

back

    on our street

           & *insurance* wasn't

  a word

  until we turned thirteen

    three boys in one

summer & old boy Cortel needed

  assurances

      we wouldn't snitch   on him   kissing

Brittney Brown in that stairwell

        where the walls were our fresco

of put-out ash on newly lit cigarettes

      & infinite rips & coughing

fits   of pink

    throats. We gutted

spliffs stolen   cigarillos copious

tobacco dandruff thick   in the hair of stairwell carpet

  we smoked it   to the filter.

    You was born right there Shawn pointed at a stain

on the second floor

    stair   flight

    his smoke in my eyes

  & and we burnt it

                bare   feet

                        had it out   elbow

& fist

            until my face was the anonymous paste

                                    of my own afterbirth

& after

            we spoke only with our chins

                        until they grew wires

            of black hair

& at eighteen I caught Shawn

            fucking

Cortel's Brittney   Brown & bare ass

            in that stairwell.

& not till today

            have I talked

cause

            Cortel still lives

                    in that stairwell

& Shawn became that cop

            & I know I'm not

the only boy

            who dreams

                                unbound

a lifted moment

from the top rung

of our complex

one final

flight.

—

What I Uncovered

When I was so much
younger than you, or even
first memories of salt water,
my o bachan, little grandmother
Matsumi, told me her name held
the warning of wave rush: tsunami.
t – s – u – n – a – m – i She was called
Matsumi because her father found her alive,
blue but breathing, on the seafloor. There is one wave,
says my grandmother, *bigger*
than a rich man's house, bigger
than a poor man's appetite, bigger
even than a tender woman's smile. There
is a wave so high it grows the length of a full day
to reach our island. It swallows up all the water in Japan
to build itself. It swallows the note of every birdsong to build
itself. It swallows even the sun to shape itself so high it scrapes
the roof of heaven, then we fisher's people come to see what's bare
on seafloor: shell and fish and shark—old boat and new wedding ring
—a thousand children's toys—sometimes even a baby girl held inside lips
of ocean floor—where my father found me, like a pearl—his pearl, his Matsumi.

> I asked my mother,
> *Did that really happen?*
> "Absolutely not," she said,
> "Everyone who left home to see the seafloor

before the tsunami was pulverized or drowned.
That was just some old poem."

A poem, I thought.

—

Of What America: How to Assemble a (1) Native (2) Nippon (3) Cubana Body in (4) Appalachia

My burnt body hangs crisscross over beach dunes

below where family gathers children's ringing

sand laps toys tangled in teenage lust the skin consciousness

potential of everyone eyeing one another in sunbursted bottoms

there is nothing here but the bliss of this day

& so I think on death

hanging out over the Pacific so many

dead

       mi familia

       watashi kazoku

       kwaji'ya'

       my kinfolk

there are four ways to name the century of dying in me

what passions grew a mixed-mixed skinned boy

who would plant his body here & witness

a happy beach rooted in the smile of so much

untilled history somewhere far the open

ocean ferried my padre between Cuba

& Miami swam pescado inside each swell of lung

unmoored he said until his mind *fell into love*

with the woman who fled America's

internment camps a pregnant Nippon

daughter's flight from San Diego

to Somerset, PA tegami kaku yo

I'll write you letters she touched

the shovel shaped incisors of a Native

American boy whose floorboards were still

booting the reeducation each hode'noda'

song of defacto fathers my Onondaga origin

bowed beneath the whip

of whiteness lashed he laid down

love for my kin who ran skinny rail

lines what split Appalachian silt & marl

my feet saddle all the loosed

mud of so many continents

where everyone is gone

somedays

& somedays they aren't

because I believe on

days like this

with a mouthful of expiring

sun the potential of

a small beginning

what sustains a soul

across imagined borders

what finds

tortured bodies

their song

of forward

rejoicing.

The Lion   The Witch   & My Brother Timiko

We're well past   your wardrobe
& on hospital steps.   You've jumped
from our mother's   40mph minivan

for a third time   this month. I beg
& explain   a concept high above
the black hair   on your head I shaved

it so many times   to the bareness: analogy
the Lion   is in your heart. & the Witch
doesn't ride backseat   in our mother's

Chevy Lumina.   Tumbling though across
your face it's obvious   you've eaten all
the Turkish delight   chased Kool-Aid smile.

They say Down syndrome   is
a continuum.   but we've ridden all the way
to Narnia for years   & arrived right here. Parked

our carriage so far   from the beautiful

British schoolchildren   on VHS you love

sometimes I wonder   if it'd be easier

for me to force   a flea market sword

through the white chest   of a real ice witch

anything to bring you with us   back home.

Run: 2nd Street   Harrisburg PA   Summertime '17

Bullshit   watch your sister   be arrested

for daring   to dance   her jay-stunting

across the street   be next   to her but say

nothing   because this ain't   Footloose

and you will   always be   a coward

instead just be   thankful   for the iphones

filming   for women   with stronger

forearms   for men   with bigger

voices   think instead about   your next

drink   don't be   thinking

about   every other   time

you were   not   brave

don't be   thinking   *I am a teacher*

sometimes   I even smile   at cops

I can win   this one over   with kind reason

he is bald   white   short

his uniform   has come   untucked

be close   enough   to see cliché

sweat   on his upper lip   be brave

be brave   you think   about anything but

boot scrape   baton clatter   police-grade

mace   your own knee's   crunch

against storefront   signpost   stumbling away

I could be   blind   what if I am

blind   forever   you think

why am I   mouthing   *Excuse me Sir?*

I Can't Close My Eyes Without Seeing Jason Pero's Body

Boys like us don't make national news.
That's what we'd tell each other, fleeing

the long blue arms of police LEDs.
Our hightop Reeboks kissed gravel

miles of Central Pennsylvania Street. Us
not old enough to have kissed a lover. Boys

like us, cops shoot & ask questions never,
we laughed. We ran. We laughed. We hollered

"PIG!" as if it was just another pickup game
of basketball on blacktop. We were so young—

how young is too young to teach a boy never
turn his index finger & thumb into the hammered steel

of a gun. *You might die.* I breathe for decades,
older & older & now when I close my eyes

I can see Jason Pero isn't with us boys—us running
from cops. Jason is at home. *He was a teddy bear,*

said his grandpa. *He teased his little nephews once
in a while but that was the meanest part he had.*

Jason Pero is in his front yard making the best
of our Bad River Reservation, turning porch boughs

into a drum set, each stick cracking stained wood.
He imagines making it all the way to high school

drumline. & here comes that cop with report
"of a man carrying a knife." & here is Jason drumming.

& here there will be no justice for death, no video
evidence of Jason's dying. Just this one that plays out

endlessly in my head. The greatest horror
writers know it's worse when you can't see the monster:

jaws that catch, claws that bite, hidden just off screen.
In Onondaga, our clan mother says kahséhtha' *I hide*

something akweriákon in my heart. But tonight, I am done
with hiding. Jason Pero was shot once in the shoulder

& once *in the heart*. & my heart beats faster the longer
I sleep. The longer I close my eyes. The longer we hide.

Split the Lark   & You Will   Find the Music

In the spring   of my first leaving   an Onondaga longhouse

two men tried   to kill themselves   what little was left

of their souls   whipsawed ringside   & res-sanctioned lights

blistered a mixed   crowd all of it   just another town scraped

out the prairie   Monongahela   whos-it-whats-its jostling

for a look   through scribbled   sight toward the sparkle

of two men's   encaged torsos   *we are better than this?*

asked the woman   next to me   smelling so sweetly of strawberries

it would almost make   a sick stomach   hunger

NO EYES   NO DICK KICKS   & NO GRABBING HOGS

yelled the scared   Crow of an officiator   all but ignored

by the two men   of muscle & leopard   born supple

now rigid   in their arms   jack-in-the-boxes of unsprung

potential how many   bodies are built   upon the strong

foundations of pain   ours rang red   with the chorus of a butcher's

floor spilled   bucket tossed tooth   & snout on oil-slick mats

here are the so-called tree loving   hippies us   vines around the trunk

of violence   Natives against our own   selves the smaller

fighter's teeth   knocked jagged   as a fresh kilned key

& now I see   he is just a boy   stumbling the man

next to me shouts   *a hurt dog barks*   whatever the fuck that means

before the scores   are tallied I skip   out on the worst parts of myself

when I drive home   I shake so hard   I can barely hold the steering

& when I reach   for the door of my last night   in this home

I cannot   remember why   I decided to leave the fight

How to Break a Horse for Riding

The gentle say a hard break
does not take because even beasts
remember the whip.

But every rich man will tell
you the gentle are poor
in more than spirit.

If a horse will not kneel
for a rider
starve it.

Hunger will bring even
a proud man to heel
at your boots.

Saddle a colt in its youth
load it with a heavy enough burden
to buckle its knees.

Then when you mount him
the weight of a grown man will seem
less than the whole world.

When you ride what is yours
steer him down any untrod path
everywhere you desire.

If you break him surely
then he is yours
never to be returned corner store.

If you know that I am the horse
please remember
I was once just a boy.

More Precious Than Pizza

It is only twenty-five years
ago—you are six and a half
and halfway through your
very own personal pan
pizza—little bodies build
into straight lines inside the
Elementary   cafeteria—
grease on your small
fingers—grease on your t-
shirt collar—your small legs
wobble in a small chair—
and a big big bronze medal
dangles by a bright yellow
sash around your neck—
and that medal is big as
your fist—and that medal is
gleaming—today—it says
BOOK IT!—and you're
worth a million bucks—
today—medal   day—
ceremony day—you'd read
sixteen books just this
month—you   didn't
cheat— Toby did— Zach
might   have—Chelsea

did—definitely—not you
though—you are six and a
half and now you've had
your pizza and you still
have the medal for today
and tomorrow and the
next day—there's nothing
better than wearing a
medal every day.

Tomorrow you're in the
cafeteria with your medal
and your small hands are
clean and your legs are
wobbling and you are
hungry—but still worth
close to a million
bucks tomorrow—now
tomorrow—you're in the
cafeteria with your medal
and your small hands are
clean but shaky and you
are very hungry—and you
realize you aren't worth

quite as much as public school lunch costs—the memory of pizza grease is nowhere—but your shirt collar—so when Toby sits next to you oh you are small—small hands small legs—you are never smaller than now—now today when you hand him your medal—a trade—no take backs—his brown paper bag—for your big big bronze BOOK IT! medal—and when you open the bag—when you open the bag there is note from a mother—with a heart—and there is a careful sandwich— and a favorite blue spoon— and a name brand dessert— and you find more love in that brown paper bag—than you ever will in medals.

—

Tesso The Iron Rat, God of Broken Promises

Many of my brothers killed in the trenches were buried exactly where they fell.
Often we had to dig in deeper, and decomposing bodies were everywhere. Corpses
attracted rats. Just two rats can give birth to a thousand offspring a year, and
soon our trenches swarmed with disease.
—Haruto Takahashi, Nisei in American Uniform

After the war   my ojiisan slept so deep   a child dare never
knock the ritual   of his waking   feared summon of the yokai
split demon   from the far Land   of Rising Sun
bolted bedroom   door behind three locks   lathered thick
such red dripping   paint coated even   the twin hinges of lynch pins
this Buddhist supplication   to Tesso   rat demon god of rats
vertically inked   down its ruby face   when my eyes were curious
enough to read English   my grandmother translated   each slashed character

TESSO   GOD OF RATS   DO NOT ENTER
I   I   I
AM   AM   AM
SORRY   SORRY   SORRY

why I asked   my grandmother   will this god not forgive grandpa
a good god   forgives   I learned in Sunday school
I would not   understand   a broken oath made so far away
from an American god   the rat god far from our home   in Somerset, PA

she said   in one summer she heard   mourning birdsong
trapped inside the silver grip   of our gutters   she hoisted me up
armed with a spade   I was to free   what was caged
I fished through wet   nests and still pink   blossoms of spring forgotten
on splintered eggshells   I shoveled   into a wriggling
mass   the grey length   of a rat giant larger
than my spade   and a cry the length   of my prepubescent body
and my fall   was the exhale of a small boy's   prayer
where in air   I saw a window   into my grandfather's opening
of a curtain   his room   littered with rat traps unsprung
maws of iron   the jagged teeth of cages   empty of life
save my ojiisan   awoken by the early morning   clamor above
I fell through   the halls of that house for years   before his death
when I begged   my grandmother to speak   of the rats
your ojiisan broke   an oath I cannot   repeat she said
I will unlock that door   when you are old enough   to know war
and before I was a man   to ask   one more time she died
and the unknown   has demoned me   more than any knowing ever could
but I understand now   as a man   she would never have told me
and it is better this way   for a man to have never known   war

$19.42

Japanese Internment photo:
Family outside   Home
American   flag in frame
NO JAPS   WANTED
in red   In red a mother's elbow
stained   against windowsill
Here this ink of my ancestry

for sale on Ebay.

$19.43

Japanese Internment photo:
Black and white   banner a mother
points pale   above her home. JAPS
KEEP   MOVING
THIS   IS A WHITE MAN'S
NEIGHBORHOOD   Her sign
still drying   wind beaten
Here this ink of my ancestry

for sale on Ebay.

$19.44

Japanese Internment photo:
Five women huddled   around a game
of Go   dark stone pieces
each barracked   woman
watches   the jagged quartz
guards piecemeal   in uniform
roll call   on a clipboard
Here this ink of my ancestry

for sale on Ebay.

Insecticide

a white man
   lived high
   on a hill
     & he called
     us boys
        his
      beetle boys
      down
    the block
   & every word was
true

Nick sneakered
   the pedals
   Jason straddled
     the pegs
     & me
       in the front basket
       like some
      overgrown ET
    it was summer
    & we were seven
  but we knew
  how to bike
up hills

we were his
    when he paid
    us two weeks
        in a row
        half a penny per
            japanese
            beetle
                copper shine
        he called us
        sometimes
    so *copper shine*
    we called the field
of his backyard
    emeralds of opportunity
alive in our palms

capital
    was our
    -ism was a man
        who watched us
        out a big clear window
            his beetle boys
        our shirtless buzz
        our delicate wings
        what led us
    closer
    to his home
every day

"Bonfire-flies,"

my daughter calls them
into the tiny moons
of her outstretched palms

summer's spilled song
courts her every imagination
alighting on our lawn

watquœntowáno jotécka
her grandmother names them
big-bellied fires from the porch

jotécka! jotécka! jotécka!
my daughter squeals dancing
barefoot by the drum of her heart

tonight she tastes the fire
of each clipped consonant
the light of Onondaga on her tongue

she dances faster than flames
bonfire wings aflutter
at the edges of her little pajamas

I pray her whole
life she will call her own jotéka
breathe fire like this from heaven

just another   horse poem

a filthy little indian   that's what she calls me
this stallkeep half woman   half corncob pipe
my ears smoke red   every time she huffs filthy
but I tamp down   my tongue quick
cause she lets me muck   stall after stall
better to smell like a horse   than an Indian
if I say *ain't that the truth*   she'll laugh and leave
she'll wade out   into blinding pasture
so far I can barely see   all the shadows
of what tangles her   she'll stand scarecrow
for hours smoothing down   her own matted hair
while I dare run   my fingers slick with spittle
through the base knot   after knot of one sweet boy
and his sticky mane   *if you touch him I will beat you*
redder than your Cherokee hide   I nod knowing
there are times to joke   and times to nod
at night when I sneak in   *sweet boy* nods to me
between pipe bars   black stall after stall
lit by a pitcher of moonshine   and the shimmer
of his milky huff   my big toothed *agonze agonze*
I know where *agonze*   all the keys are hid
I sing sweet   boy *agonze* his true name
he nods   nods and nods until my arms

are mottled in his hide   until he lies down
and I paint myself   across the musculature
of his back   and when he stands tall
I let my hands lie long   behind the pieces
of his shoulders and when I   hold the wet drum
of his heart   I am ne hochsàte I am
horsemen fullhearted   enormous I am
I am clean I am I am   bigger even than this moment

Ode to the Three Herniated Disks in My Back

to write this, clear
I swallowed the pain
of not chewing my tongue
or the entire bottle of addiction,
doctor prescribed. I think,
therefore I am in pain. Our proof
of reality is suffering. In Japanese
we say good things always come in
3's & 5's, & that must be
why I ruptured
triplets down the slide
of my spine. Sacrum popped, is it
true I'll only ever have one
lumbar—what's the word
for when even
your skeleton begs
to escape you?

Pass the Rock

We called him Larry Bird
        because he was
the only white boy
        who'd play with us. Like rain he was
everywhere
        fluvial
& clear & lithe & light-
        footed, he was uncorked
champagne by a mouth
        of blacktop.
Boy wore the hell out
        of green every Wednesday night
& shamrocked
        us; beat the breaks
off us; & we hurt him for it:
        emblems of blood
spatter
        on his jersey; his eye
elbow-blackened for a week; knees
        splintered over
& again. The real reason
        we called him our "Hick
from French Lick,"

was because he'd play hurt,
our no-complaints Larry Bird—just dance
        after every easy layup
light-
        hearted through every uncalled foul:
he was always in
        flight.
I'm south of okay he'd say
        but far north of cancer.
& we loved him.
        & I loved him.

Doodle of a Yankee Dandy Family

Always   on the other side   of town
folks homes   smelled   Yankee candle
strong   Fresh Cotton   Lake Sunset
Sweet Candies   Sparkling   Cinnamon
Bahama Breeze   Fireside   God Bless
America   Spirit of U.S.A.   spent brass
stacked bodies   we called it white   reek
the spoor   of what   we could never afford
booking it   down their   clean streets
swept intentions   the pure   pulse of heart
in our eyeing   the light   behind all
their unsmudged   windows   families set
for supper   we skidded   curbside
fisted rocks   it's true   we weren't creatives
yet   we hucked   our youngblood the shout
our fingers   boundless   rocket our wrist
now elbow   shoulder   whatever weight
was unloosed within   centered   in our backs
shot forward   to bite the glass   fragment
the hearth   of every happy   family's ending

"Onirche."

I give you over

        says my brother
        upon discovering
        via social media

I am seeing
a white woman

                my only
                blood—

Onirche

        to speak it Onondaga
        is to speak it eternal
        is to speak it anima

I give you over

           to Ohàra
           to Flint
        to our people's Death

Blood—

> *You are no longer*
> *my blood*

says jatattége
my shared blood brother

I give you over

> *to Ògera*
> to Snow
> to your Snow Woman.

| *Would you* | *hate yourself?* |
| I want | to say |

| *Would you* | *hate yourself?* |
| forever | brother |

| *Would you* | *hate yourself?* |
| for want | of warmth |

| *Yes,* | *forever* |
| my brother | says |

I give you over

                to winter

to white men

           the long snow

of soldiers

who   *razed*

our bodies

who   *sodomized*

our land

who   *pillaged*

our pride

all

                for pelts

for a kind

                of warmth

of warmth

Itsy-Bitsy

Brown body knitted through
the white webbing.

The infinite geometric proofs

are not mathed or equated
by any man's minding.

Only we are
watching the predator spool prey

my daughter & me & her
wriggle against my chest.

She reaches toward the venom
of what she does not know

would surely kill her.

A small death of vessels
& each organ within

her tiny abdomen
my everything.

I was singing a song to her
one she insists

I made up
about the itsy bitsy.

A baby girl who would climb
every water spout

& the rain & the rain
would be everywhere

blue in spring & summer
she falls into new clothes

the knitted silk
of a spider's song,

what helps put her to sleep.

Will one day puncture the soft flesh
of my tongue

every lullaby can wring
itself into a final cry

though from so far away
you don't know

if it's mine
or my daughter's

or no one
at all.

—

Sons of Cain

Kentucky sky flints
      the steel of storm heads
blue fields
      our intentions
black I hurl the axe handle
      all nine years of my elbow
into the bowl
      of my brother's orbital
socket crack &
      thunder his good eye
consumed
      he screams
& I sprint
      field-long & ducking
each rock he throws
      shears the soft heads
of bluebells
      his rage outruns my fear
& when he catches
      me with an orange of stone
caught in the crepuscular
      muscle of wind
braids our long hair skyward
      he crushes my shoulder
& long limbed I catch
      his neck in the hollow
of my arm & the rain
      speckles us purple
inside sheaves

                   of tall grass
wind song
                   his body's breath pinned
beneath what muscle
                   I have grown
into the silence
                   of that dawn
the downpour
                   of his stoppered breathing
& before I understand
                   it is as if we are
in embrace
                   when his body gives
limp
                   to my chest
there I walk up a hill
                   & look down
on my brother
                   the body
of his eighth summer
                   the earth spins
itself slow until
                   he wakes & I go
down to him & weep
                   in his arms
How did we get
                   all the way out here?
he asks.

Annuli

I am on my knees, and he wants me
to place the horns here on my head, he
presses between my eyes. Wide, the ram horns
heavy, my shoulders buck—forward as I proffer
the skull, antlers twined, trumpeted rust
of war sways, high as a boy my stature can. *Reach!*
You are a Stone sheep, says my grandfather you
small horned, brown lamb, but not much
longer—
He steers the horns and curls, his palms
around what is already curled. *I killed*
this Dall ram when he was thirteen, just a morsel
older than you, says grandfather. Ram's jawbone
digging into my forehead, *you can tell*
a sheep's age by the annuli, each ring
three seasons full of growth, he says, ringed fingers
scraping the thin hair of my forearms. He pulls
his fingernails through the keratin, carves through
both horns and it hails clippings of bone
where beetles bed down, where I kneel
on red carpet. *You can feel the ages beneath*
each finger, he says and now I recall forever:
the timbre of his voice breathing, *someday*
you will be a great hunter of beasts—
hunter of men. And now I kneel as a man,
neck bowed with the weight
of each season and how I could not escape
the yoke of a beast's horns.

7:34 A.M.'s Basement: Wabash Avenue

Ten years past   arcade lights exorcised
plinked and pulled   each neon demon
from the knot   of your pubescent back
here you are again   kneeling at the altar
of a rumbling   game late to work you pray
to the small   god of washing machines
of patrons who have   forgotten
or let go   or passed over the silver
shine of a stray   twenty-five cents
you need to make it   all the way
to a dollar fifty   enough change
will make your white shirt   whiter
so you won't be   fired
this time   you won't be fazed by prick
by glass by lint   by now you've stained
your knees your slacks   on yesterday's
damp but for the span   of a concrete slab
you'll stretch   each finger further
you'll find   that quarter
you'll let yourself   consider
this small posture   of a child holy.

Humanity in the Corpse of a Whale: When We're Done Eating / Each Other / Is All That Will Be / Left

Kuskokwim Bay.
Chill nearly artic,
copper broth of sun ladles
the mega fauna carcass in heat:
a rotten humpback whale, beached her
once-rough hide soft yellow, orange even
blacked by days of isolated
dawn.

Still, in death
she is longer than any school bus filled
with children's singing, but inside
her, the scullery of unlocked chest cavity, here
is the wet tear and purr
of a single mother
grizzly bear.

Alaskan rain flashes white among her tracks

so far north, yet even the cliff faces
bend at the ferocity of rolling muscles emerged
from daylight feasting.

A mother's fur is the flush of petrified
wood, slicked back in the glue of dried and dripping
gore. Oil-gummed and grizzly-eyed, she stumbles
to find her children. There is still hope
her full body will be
a second meal
bite by bite.

Truth or Dare

all black cows   pitch in the night

beetly bugs   sizzle as steam

above the nape   of their sleep

mouths clatter   with the full snap

of human teeth   there is no voice

in this field but us   my legs grown

out the tall grass   barefoot

a crept boy   shot out unskyed night

I leap for the high   tale weavers

of myth I'll speak   myself legend born

my small butt   womps against the skeleton

of an Auberdeen Angus   her moo

not the slow drawl   of movies but urgent

peal hooved bone   she balks my frame

stratosphere   where I meld with the cloud

of bugs infinite eyes   symbiotic her starry pupils

are moonwise   with the easy truth

of my calve years   what possesses a boy

to dare   the hulk of all dormant nature

The Whine of a Father

I am just like my father. A factory man who never could make it
to the factory, but cleaned, gutted, packed deer like there were jewels
inside, like there wasn't a Food Lion who'd lick and glue
our food stamps two blocks down. He'd disappear on a hunting trip—
me and my brother alone for a week left only with cereal. *An arrow's*
whistle, just the whistle, can tell a deer you're coming, he'd say.
After, we would eat cold venison for weeks. He took me just once,
hunting: we sat in a wet rut and nothing came, deer or doe.

I am just like my father. Before dawn, tender words rustle bobtails,
even, I remember the whistle of my arrow will startle them. But,
when I loose myself, heel to head, across the forest I am never
myself, but the arrow—piercing between foreleg and rib. Where
I wish there was song there is always the knowing
whine of death. My father in our bathroom. Faucet running, he
remembers my mother, and the whistle of his throat
is everywhere.

180 Pope Lick Road, Somewhere Kentucky

I been traveling / I been traveling from toe to toe
Everywhere I have been / I find some old Jim Crow
—Huddie Ledbetter "Leadbelly," *Jim Crow Blues*

I was younger than the cherry branch / lacquered table my daddy slammed / Miller High Lifes off that sixer / of a summer night / he introduced me to a genuine cowpuncher / "Jesse here wrangles cattle" said my daddy / cowboy tipped his hat / "little young for a dive bar, arent'cha?" he said / and I couldn't hear over the gleam / of his DIXIE / belt buckle the elastic snap /of mud-stained suspenders / "speak up, boy / you deaf?" growled my daddy into his can / Almighty Lord, how a young boy yearns to be / a cowboy / my ears went red / "boy's awfully dark / to be yours" said the cowpoke and spit / and no sooner his spittle gladdened floorboards / than my daddy stood a full pair / of overalls shorter than the man / "who're you calling / dark?" / said my daddy / and the cowboy strolled bar-side / smiling / and that's the first time I seen my daddy / stand on my account / and later the alley reeked of cherry / puke and we saw the cowboy / vomit a gallon / into his 30oz hat / "probably too many / pink margaritas" said my daddy / together we laughed / and together we started up the truck / then found another / bar.

Ode to My Once & Future Alcoholism

We cradled El Yucateco
        on our tongues
until the loser cried
    tío!
& numbed
        over green
glassed bottles
        our uncles laughed

        in Elementary
halls we tongue tied
        ourselves
with Atomic Fireballs
        & at home
cinnamon
        toothpaste scrubbed
our cut gums

sleepovers were
        spiced hours spent
shoving packets
        of Big Red full
jawed we tongued
        silver wrappers
affixed our foreheads
        with fire
you bitch
        we shouted at whoever
won out
        through the pain

We traded up
to Middle School
        gum for Listerine strips
older kids said
        an entire green packet
can make your tongue
        bleed
& they weren't wrong

& after our tongues
        we bled out
for plastic bottles
        of Cool Mint
liquid handles
        torn from shelves
the mouthwash
        pooled our stomachs
antiseptic we stumbled
        drunk
for the first time
        full of green
shine & sure
        enough none of us
ever got a goddamn
        cavity
but what we did
        get got us
it got us good.

Irish Spring

is what they called   the crop
circle of our trailer   park its spindling
series of disposable homes   tin cylinders
hitched only to the plinked memory   of rain
watered by the teething   saliva of 100 white babies
oh by all the fucking   catholic gods
irish or otherwise how i wanted   to be one of them
a white baby   swaddled in anonymity
trust me no amount of lathering   rinse after rinse of irish spring
could wash off all of my color   "little beast"
they called me fire side   in lawn chairs & overturned logs
rotten & bark peeled   i prayed to be cleansed by their gods
but life for a child   is a passive verb
so i fought wild hair   black beneath sun
blackened the eyes   of a dozen white boys
peeled them as a burn   shed from the back of my neck
my back burns   with the memory of their father's leather
burns with the memory   of their son's baby teeth lodged under
my 1st & 2nd knuckle   scars became the white pride
that shined across my flesh   hallelujah praise a white god
burn black the memories   every fuckin one.

|Diptych|

doble	songs
of rejoicing	una vez
a vessel	for monsters
considers	what too we axed
all that was	split to feed
the fire	loss
of all	lost things
found	one another

—

Lungs Full of Oil

For ages
I have seen
        my sisters paddle
        through cities
flowing
without
        a single blue river
        for ages
I have seen
my brothers hunt
        their own
        ghosts unending
forests shorn
cinders
        our First Nation
        our extinction
I have seen
for ages
        White men
        lay down
glittering miles
of pipeline
        lay down
        laws to purchase
the very air
in our lungs
        they say
        lay down
for a second
American

> genocide
> *lay down*

for ages
they say

> *lay down.*
> *lay down.*

Sehiàrak: Remember It

Principal   Keary Mattson examined the medicine
pouch and removed some of the   ceremonial
tobacco as Kaquatosh   cried
    —INDIAN COUNTRY   TODAY

Thank America's God   one less medicine pouch
threatens the hallways   of a public middle school
shouts a country   finger to the forehead
of our Native   face. A thirteen-year-old

Menominee girl   should not be armed enough
for prayers   of peace *I pray four times*
a day Rose Kaquatosh   told reporters. Report
the news: whiteness   wears an army

of crosses. Each   gold neck precious
with metal   shine where the hammer found home
in overturned wrists   this tribute to violence
daylight's hanging. Bring   anything

save the medicine pouch   she who heals
your tired and sick. Bring anything   but medicine
for they poor   in more than spirit
hang them   by the neck by a cross by gold.

Bare Neck of the Woods

My ma
           said agony
said hurt
           said she'd be
damned
           if pain
ain't the one
           thing all folk
say's true
           says all folk bow
when pain
           huck
her elbow
           across they neck
all folk
           kneel
when pain
           bite
dog-sure
           at the belly
of old knees
           when pain
rolls through
           this town
even the trees
           burst
at the seams
           she said.

Any How's Course

here
is a photo
a polaroid
      of course
(could it be
      anything else)
stuck
on white
refrigerator
      of course
(could it be
      anyplace else)
this snapping
shot
of my young
father
      of course
(could it be
      anyone else)
supcrimposed
by sawdust
by sun
by mourning
      of course
(could it be
      anytime else)
dipping

the whine
of a chainsaw
deep in brown
flesh
      of course
(could it be
      anykind else)
of fallen
oak
that day
he made his own
father's casket
      of course
(could it be
      anywhy else)
on his cremation
on this day
i drop
this vignette
into another
dark box
wondering
of course
(could it have been
      any other way)

Between Porch Boughs a Real Hasgaragéchte[1] and His Onondaga Son

spring grass
gives way
beneath an age
of sickle men
us too
blades
bent
this night
it is clear

I have kept
the bending
of myself
in-two
everything
my father
hates
the softness
of touch
the fullness
of a circle
the full bend
of a man
without
edges

---

[1] Man of War

Count me. Number me. The First shall be

7. Today

                 you are

      seven (& you

identify

      I am

in second

      2. person) today

not the first

           1. person pulled

by a Sunday

      mother down through

today's forest

             church pew after

pew stained by others

      6. waiting on salvation

today nails & wood

             are in the palms

of the part-time

      Bible man

Go ask him

             ask him

for salvation

      says my mother

& I hesitate

                                today she says

today & I hesitate
            & I wait
in that splintered
                        line today for a savior
for 3. years I wait
                                    in line
for 4. years I wait
                        for salvation
I wait as a footnote
                        as a tittled jot
between 5. verses
            & the line grows
longer the longer
                        I wait & today I woke
up
            unnumbered
in line again & again today
                                    I woke up
maybe
            tomorrow I won't.

When My Brother Calls and Tells Me How Little Insurance Will Cover, Yes, Cancer

after

the red

republic comes

taking all

each copper button

every gold thread

of what is

threadbare

what coinage

i have stored

in strip mall

wishing wells

i wonder

is   *wealth*
the sum
of what is left
after
$0.

Living with Grandpa, 1995-1996

Tonight we truly live in
primary colors—where my
grandad takes me hand in
hand—I am not yet too old
to hold a hand—let's go see
the "jungle buzzards"—he
says "what's left of the old
hobo troop"—and we travel
from the small spine of the
country to an erupted
city—where earth grew
limb after metal limb into
black sky—"Junebug" even
in December he calls me—
"did you bring your piggy
bank?"—I tell him "No"—
paw says the homeless only
spend money on drugs—
"Your daddy five pounds of
shit in a one pound sack"—
he says and grandad ain't
never wrong.

My jacket is puffy—and it's
cold as a witch's tit—and

there are witches here beneath the storefront eaves—and they poke at me one-eyed and warty—and when I yell out—grandad laughs so loud the spell of it scares snow—off sills and like moths—we float deeper into the city lights—until we reach a big bridge and I can see—the trolls beneath—he asks me if I've heard about trickle-down economics in school—"No" I say "but I know trickle means *a little something*"—"Good" he says—"a little something can buy a lot of happiness"—and under the bridge that night—by the light of oil drums—I watched a rich soul—spill his little wealth—over so many happy faces.

The Weight of Morning

Four-cornered night,
the faucet plinks—
plinks a wet thousand's
thousand of droplets
each stood just once
to sing
upon the silver bell
of bathtub stopper.
In morning, a small
boy forms and collects
his body; he lets
it curl within
that night's work:
the abundance
of hours, each drip
drip he dreams
could once have been
a warmth. *Wait,
just wait*, he says
only himself, here
he washes
the outside:
slender legs
of inner dark.

Reasons to Cry When the Landlord Evicts You

Ignored serving suggestions
I am positively shitfaced off another
bottled Wine of the Month basket
addressed to the woman who died
in this apartment before me
I will redact her name here
out of respect for the deceased arriving
on my dream's doorstep my Ghost
of the Month Club *[Redacted], your hair is*
the color of cathedral creek— remember
that pear chardonnay you sent February.
I pour out my secrets a whole
orchard of her hinting vanilla
lace in my hands she says *I had a husband*
Remember? You've read all my letters
again and again I wake hardly Man
of the Month hungover and grasping
for painkillers for the lightness of water
for what brimming will fill me
for what brimming will fill me
for what brimming will fill me

just another   night sky poem

universe shatters   into an infinite   piece within
the great death there is   no heaven no earth   once bodied
mind has turned there is   only this   past mind cannot be
grasped   present mind cannot be   grasped future
mind   cannot be   grasped

—Dogen Zenji, Soto school of Zen founder

dear daughter   of atlas   high above high

blacked streets   blue hills   every silvering light post

see a brown dwarf   turn   rise as a dowser

from amidst deep   frost   in the lotus pond

grasp toward a constellation   of bats   ignited

in her   fanged maw   gasps overlap

look   down the pleiades   barreled in your palm

notice   the naked eidolon   of your eye sail

the path   of a fired meteorite   sutured

by black paper   cuffs   of a night shirt

dovetailed   by nursing doe   ghostly derivations

of brightest indigo   the whirr   lenticular moon-

bow   now a discus   plumbs down a wink

of green   plates atop a table   askimmer

top hats bursting with   alleyways   bustled

ladies suppering   in sunstained   tops

mind   the southern chains   gone alit

her comets   belled   rings sands of sound
slipped dirt   skips from an old   shoe
of cosmic   distance   up a ladder she reaches
atop   a suite   of stairs arrayed
parallaxes of sea   anemones   suckle
tandem   centroids eyes beneath   a galactic
brow bent   under high tide   of supernumerary
azure   in a casted arc   so much symmetry
spooling out   long   bucktail
caught   fingerling in a fishbowl   full
of hackled   lures   latched by a single mole
within a dark   circlet of hair   clove
to the sides of   star head   coupled
inside   the imprint   of your index finger

witness   beyond   a bedlam of paling light
parceled   by nothing   but bang
a whirled ocean   of kelvin   degrees
kilned   in key   hole clusters
spiraled arms   of low   ignition atop
rinds of tidal binaries   lost   in eddies of giant
blue leeches   bound   between the toes
of spindly trolls   this mountain   king
with a compass   sewn   into his side made small
clothed only   in clouds   over snowflake's
shadow   bumbling   through an ache

of hewn trees   now jagged   signposts
stick his feet   light drips   light from his heel
sprinkles   jade meated hearts   of trees
as he sets down   a bug-jeweled crown   sweeps
fingers four   knuckled across   a partial corona
sprayed matter   sparkles   the interstice between
ox horns   she who tills   white in blackest field

do not turn away   from fierce   eels writhing inside
the ragged   tunnels   dark wires
rookeries   of rain   rifling down the luminance
this final fire   at the end   of your nose
here a painted mullion   bobtails dug up   bird bones
beside the mother   bear   at her burrow
she ventures   out   toward the bowl of deep
sea catches   the fish keeps   beneath
the underbelly   of urtext twice   knotted tongue
this widowing   moment   of cobbled moments
between   waking   between forgetting

our dreams   of a language   attributed
to random   error   or signs
of scapegrace   scions   at a tinseled flywheel

—

Passing Through a Mechanicsburg Highway on Our Way to The Pediatrician

Squall   after squall   bends over the steel
carcass of our   car   a blind white lifted
temporary   blizzards   entomb what road

I cannot see   the baby   cradled in her car seat

oblivious   to every slipped mile   of death
you live   to unbuckle her   fragile & puny
& alive   & still so   so warm.

How to Love a Televangelist

for Joel Osteen

O, poor wolf:
belly pig-full,
liveried rich
in sheepskin condoms.

O, how I want
to cudgel you
with sarcasm
or cudgel

O, but
on whom do you call
when your child's
diagnosis is terminal?

O, but
to whom do you send
the money-seed to sprout
a tree of blessings?

O, but
at whose feet do you lay
the desperate work
of dying?

just another   fruit fly poem

Blossom   by a black stem
single seed   of strawberry's lust
she cusps   her mouth
at the edge   of this week's water
here   on a leaky windowsill
droplets threaten   *I'll swallow*
the new   girth of you. We share
small   delights. Crumbs
of spring   sun. Small she is
enough   to fill what cracks
in me   constellating
about   my glasses she
will never land   upon my palm
There is no   princess of flies
but in our second   week I think
she trusts   me
then I find   her upended
dead   upon the windowsill
still   I weep
for what   is worth
a poem   a love
poem for what is   worth
a love   poem.

'Ohigiŵe

Mama my vein braider / thousand year bone burner
Mama my tongue twister / thousand pronged antlers
—Marie Sioux "Buried in Teeth"

Praise the Iroquois ceremony for the dead they burn corpses
the elevated selves of wind antlered manes the pollen-blown those
whose hair find fertile earth & when we incinerate my mother
I think on this singing of familial silence into ode
to my male pattern after pattern
the baldness of a barren scalp fire tumbles what is
left of my matrilineage, Onondaga
& Japanese accursed in both cultures baldness
understood as a blight of the White Man
this contamination of my genetic cost interlopes
the tether once-taught by mother earth I beg
mercy for the high price
of Rogaine what tincture can turn
the eye of a people's heart
I am ever unbraided & the pyre
which I construct for my body
will be a scored offering
for every god who would not claim me
for every ritual sewn into my wanting
skull & shine of praise
to the god of small plagues
& embered endings. Amen.

Waiting to Get into the Lil Peep Concert at House of Blues: San Diego, October 9th 2017

> "tell me that I'm dumb
>   I love to get   numb"
> —Lil Peep (1999-2017), *Right Here*

Heaven blood
          dribbles over   bones

of ocean   white
surf   coming in again

          & again plunges
the mollymawk   sooty

over shattered glass's
shimmer   of the Pacific

her muzzled bill
          bullets past pink atmosphere

pummels the face
of water   she tosses

the lavender   girth
of squid

          sunward & steaming
limbs of shined

reflection again
          & again

          I see her toy
with the torn tentacles

of what is   surely
sentient

Damn   nature has no chill
says the child   between bites

of bubblegum ice cream
        beside me   in line

        & five streets from this
dock

The National Institutes of Heath
        imprisons chimpanzees

        in beige cages
for life entirety

Yeah   no chill
I say while

        the predator flings
the limbless   football

of squid head   high
into bright celestial

& tears it
        to ribbons of sky

of flesh
        & spent sunset

Ode to My Stretchmarks

of each
mark

        what stretches
        me

lovely
in no light

        serpentine
        age

I present
the utterly

        unamazing
        each incomplete

intimacy
of no knight

        in shining this
        soft armor

of a cheered age
pleading guilty

        again
        & over a good

time there is
just the bathwater

        no baby
        shed afterparties

aftermath of so much
deciduous skin

        on skin
        what blows

the shingles off
these sunspotted shoulders

one long night
until this weight

will be overturned
a fossil

excavated by some
tiny deity

who whispers
heads I win

tails you lose
and here I am

still rolling
fucking dice

If Love is Red, then: For Want—of Love
or
Wow!—Do That Thing You Do to My Heart

Come——rejoice into your hands—unfurl—anoint yourself—across my forehead—*each-crimson-millimeter*—is desire——treasure me—a wetter ruby—than throat blood—than the blood—of the motherfucking Lamb—than earthworms writhing—ruddy in your mane—strawberried fields where everything—real is caught in consumption—lips of dripping——fire——O. YOU. ARE. A. RADIANCE.—of cardinals—a thousand fielded songs—begging for flight—congeal against me—anoint our every hour—in rejoicing flutes—of cheap rosé——crush me to chili powder—with the miracle of your tongue—strum me—as the ribs of a beloved—Solo cup——wear me—as a blacksmith wears heat—on her arms—ode—to your ginger pubic hair—tickling my throat—caress me-caress me like the svelte belly—of Louis Viton pumps——*guzzle me*-guzzle me like Fireball—fermenting beneath wedding bells——that could someday be our own—horde me like I'm that *last* red cent—ogle me like that Baywatch one-piece—bathe me—in enough tabasco to make even Texas—blush—be my clichéd slice of cherry pie——my watermelon sunrise—held just between salvation and sin——in sweat——in *skin on skin*—I'll slip into the marbling—of your very flesh—I'll kiss your bones—tender—be my portion—of velvet smile—let laughter scrub—the sweet petals of your gums—raw—with joy—watch me roll out every goddamn carpet—you will *never* paint this town alone—Love *Love* in these last days—in this Red State of our Republic—if not you—then who?—else will.

Also by Benjamin Naka-Hasebe Kingsley:

Not Your Mama's Melting Pot

Colonize Me was printed using the fonts Adobe Garamond Pro.

www.saturnaliabooks.org